Rocky Mountain Wildflowers

A Guide for Kids

MARY L. DUBLER

Thanks for Letting me
visit your classroom!
5/31/10
Mary Dubler
Psalm 121:1-2

www.pronghornpress.org

To my husband and my best friend, who happily went on many adventures in search of wildflowers and who didn't bat an eye when I would say, "Wait, I need to get a picture of that one!"

Bear's Breeches and Arrow Leaf Senecio.

The Rocky Mountains (shaded area) go through several states, and the flowers mentioned in this book can be found in most of these states. Some of the flowers will be high up in the mountains, some in the foothills, and many will also be in the plains. You can even see wildflowers in parks and vacant lots in the cities. So look carefully, especially in the spring and summer. You will be amazed at how many different flowers you will see.

Do You LOve Wildflowers?

The Rocky Mountain States are full of beautiful wildflowers, and you can see them in fields and parks, next to lakes and rivers, and especially up in the mountains. This guide will help you identify seventy fantastic wildflowers.

When you see any of the wildflowers in this guide you can note when and where you saw them, and it will be a fun reminder of your discovery.

The author, Mary Dubler, with her Canon SLR digital camera.

Mary Dubler is a veterinarian who does technical editing and lives in Colorado. Her father passed on to her a love for photography, and she began photographing wildflowers in 1995 after heavy spring rains caused the foothills to bloom. She hopes this book will in some small way instill in children of all ages an appreciation for wildflowers, and to reflect the Creator of all the beauty we see in the Rocky Mountain region.

Alpine meadow in the Snowy Range of Wyoming.

Bright Yellow Flowers

Alpine Sunflower

This flower is also known as Old Man of the Mountain. Many of the wildflowers have unique and fun names.

Alpine flowers are usually small and not very tall since the growing season at higher altitudes is so short. One of the exceptions is the Alpine Sunflower whose blossoms are sometimes four inches across. Most of the other flowers, such as the Arctic Gentian, are much smaller.

Yellow Banner

This flower is common along roadsides and in meadows from April through July.

Bright Yellow Flowers

Mexican Hat

Sometimes wildflowers get their names because the blossoms, leaves, or other parts of the plant resemble other things. I think you can see why! Also known as Coneflower, this flower is common in grasslands and in the foothills, and can often be seen along the road.

Avalanche Lily

As the snow banks retreat in the higher elevations this flower can be one of the first to bloom in the spring, sometimes as early as April.

Bright Yellow Flowers

Sunflower

There are several varieties of Sunflowers, and they can range in height from two feet to over eleven feet. The flower heads turn to follow the sun as it passes through the sky.

Gumweed

Found in the plains and foothills, this wildflower gets its name because of the sticky white coating on the flower buds before they bloom.

Bright Yellow Flowers

Narrow-leaf Puccoon

Puccoon refers to the red to yellow dye that can come from the roots of this wildflower. It is common in dry areas on hillsides and in the plains and meadows.

Bright Yellow Flowers I Found

Be sure to write down which flower you saw, where you were, the date and anything else it will be fun to remember!

_____

_____

_____

_____

_____

_____

_____

_____

_____

_____

_____

_____

Soft Yellow Flowers

Alpine Paintbrush

The dark foliage and sometimes not-very-bright yellow color means you have to look carefully to find it among the rocks. It's an Alpine flower found up high in the mountains, usually above where trees grow (called timberline). It's colder there so these flowers grow for only a few weeks during the warmest part of the summer, usually in July and August.

Hollygrape

Also known as Oregon Grape or Mountain Holly, the leaves resemble the holly we see at Christmas. The berries are oval and dark blue. In the fall the leaves change to red or purple.

Soft Yellow Flowers

Yellow Violet

Violets are sometimes called Johnny-Jump-Ups. The yellow variety has brown stripes on the yellow petals.

Prickly Pear Cactus

Sometimes the flowers of the Prickly Pear are tinged with red. The large oval pads have sharp needles that can be up to two inches long. There are many different kinds of cactus in the Rocky Mountain region, especially in the foothills and plains of the Southwest. If the plants don't have enough rain they may not bloom for several years until a big rain comes.

Soft Yellow Flowers

Salsify

The Salsify and its seed head resemble a giant dandelion. Also known as Goatsbeard, it is commonly seen along roadsides and in fields.

Yellow Paintbrush

This variety of paintbrush is also known as the Western Indian Paintbrush.

Soft Yellow Flowers

Bracted Alumroot

This wildflower likes to grow among the rocks, and its leaves sometimes turn red in the fall.

Antelope Brush

There are many types of flowering shrubs in the mountains, foothills, and plains. Most of them flower early in the spring. Antelope Brush can live on rocky soil, and to get enough water it sends out a taproot that may be up to fifteen feet long.

Common Evening Primrose

There are several different Primrose flowers, and most are either yellow or white, although you can find pink ones, too. Evening Primroses open late in the afternoon or early evening to attract the night-flying moths. The blossoms often wither the next morning.

Leafy Cinquefoil

Cinquefoil flowers are very common and there are several varieties. The word "cinque" means "five" and refers to the number of petals on this flower. When you see a flower like this you can figure out what kind of Cinquefoil it is by looking at the leaves and stems and by noting the elevation where the plant is found.

Soft Yellow Flowers I Found

Be sure to write down which flower you saw, where you were, the date and anything else it will be fun to remember!

_____

_____

_____

_____

_____

_____

_____

_____

_____

_____

_____

Peachy Pink/Salmon Flowers

Alpine Sorrel

This is an Alpine flower, but can also be found at lower elevations, where its growing season is longer. It needs more moisture, so it may grow out of rock crevices where water has collected.

Veiny Dock

This is also known as Wild Begonia. It likes sandy soil and flowers in the spring and early summer in the plains and foothills.

Butter 'n' Eggs

Many wildflowers are named after foods. This is probably one of the more unusual ones. If you use your imagination this starts to look like a fried egg with some dripping butter.

Queen's Crown

This flower is similar to King's Crown only is lighter in color. It can be up to a foot tall and has thick fleshy leaves. It likes moisture, so it may be in marshy areas up in the mountains.

Peachy Pink/Salmon Flowers i Found

Be sure to write down which flower you saw, where you were, the date and anything else it will be fun to remember!

_____

_____

_____

_____

_____

_____

_____

_____

_____

_____

Pink Flowers

Dwarf Clover

This is one of those very small Alpine flowers. It's usually only about two inches high, and the flowers have little to no stem.

Simpson Hedgehog Cactus

This small ball-shaped cactus has many sharp spines in a star pattern. During dry times it becomes dormant and can shrink below the surface of the soil.

Pink Flowers

Twinflower

This beautiful flower looks like bell-shaped lanterns hanging from a Y-shaped stem that is only about four inches tall. The Twinflower has a very sweet scent that strengthens in the evening.

Wax Currant

This shrub has flowers that can vary from white to pink, and it produces red waxy berries that birds and other wildlife like to eat.

Showy Milkweed

This plant is very common in ditches along the roads and at the edges of fields. When the stems or leaves are broken a white milky liquid comes out; this is why it is named Milkweed.

Lanceleaf Springbeauty

As the name suggests, this flowers is one of the earliest ones to bloom, often when there is still snow on the ground. It can be found in the foothills and lower valleys. The Native Americans used to dig up the roots and eat them as we would potatoes.

Pink Flowers I Found

Be sure to write down which flower you saw, where you were, the date and anything else it will be fun to remember!

_____

_____

_____

_____

_____

_____

_____

_____

_____

_____

Bright Pink Flowers

Red Clover

Several wildflowers we see in the Rocky Mountain area are also found in other parts of the country, and some have been chosen by states to be its state flower. The Red Clover is the state flower of Vermont.

Rosy Pussytoes

Although there are several different kinds of Pussytoes in the Rocky Mountain area, the Rosy Pussytoes is one of the few that has a color other than white or tan. This one is found at lower elevations, and so it may be seen as early as May.

Bright Pink Flowers

Wild Rose

This is the state flower of Iowa. It is very common in the plains and foothills. You will often see it along trails.

Old Man's Whiskers

This flower is also called Pink Plume or Prairie Smoke. It blooms early, often in May or June. There are three nodding flower stalks and the whole plant is covered with fine hairs.

Bright Pink Flowers
i Found

Be sure to write down which flower you saw, where you were, the date and anything else it will be fun to remember!

_____

_____

_____

_____

_____

_____

_____

_____

_____

_____

_____

Pinky-Lavender Flowers

Pasque Flower

This is the state flower of South Dakota. It starts blooming in May and June.

Alpine Laurel

This flower is also called Mountain Laurel. It likes cold moist areas, so you might see this one when there is still some snow on the ground.

Pinky-Lavender Flowers

Shooting Star

These drooping flowers with the bent-back petals can be pink to purple. Also known as the American Cyclamen, this unique wildflower likes shady cool spots and can bloom as early as April in lower elevations.

Gayfeather

The Gayfeather grows in dry, sandy places such as beside the road. It blooms later in the season, usually from July through October.

Pinky-Lavender Flowers

Wild Iris

Seen in sometimes large patches in moist ditches and at the edges of lakes, this flower blooms from May to July from the foothills to the subalpine areas.

Fairy Slipper

This is one of several wild orchids that grow in the Rocky Mountain region. It is also known as the Calypso Orchid and is one of the earliest to bloom, sometimes as early as April. Each plant has only one oval leaf, and it likes to grow in shady moist spots such as under pine trees.

Pinky-Lavender Flowers i Found

Be sure to write down which flower you saw, where you were, the date and anything else it will be fun to remember!

_____

_____

_____

_____

_____

_____

_____

_____

_____

_____

_____

_____

Purple-Blue Flowers

Elephanthead Lousewort

Can you see the elephant's trunk in this beautiful purple flower? Look at the close-up below. This flower also is called Elephant Flower. I have seen a whole field of these flowers in Colorado. Do you also see the Yellow Paintbrush?

Purple-Blue Flowers

Blue Flax

These flowers are on long and slender stems that can be as high as two feet tall.

Harebell

Several wildflowers include "bell" in the name and the flowers resemble bells in all kinds of shapes. There are several varieties of Harebells, and these can be found at all elevations.

Purple-Blue Flowers

Purple Fringe

This flower looks like some sort of strange pincushion. Sometimes the flowers can also be pink.

Sugar Bowl

This plant can be up to two feet tall with a single, large bell-shaped flower that is two to three inches long.

Purple-Blue Flowers

Colorado Columbine

The classic purple and white Columbine is the state flower of Colorado. Wild Columbine can also be all white, all purple, red and white, or yellow.

Jacob's Ladder

This plant has an unpleasant odor, but the bees like its beautiful flowers. The flowers can also be a pale blue with a bright yellow to orange ring inside the base.

Purple-Blue Flowers

Skullcap

This plant is sometimes hard to spot as the flowers are somewhat small. They are commonly found in the plains and on hillsides, and they bloom from May to July.

Early Larkspur

Larkspur is one of several Rocky Mountain wildflowers that is poisonous to animals. The "spur" is the pointy part coming from the back of the flower.

Purple-Blue Flowers

Western Spiderwort

This wildflower gets its name from the thick slime that oozes from broken stems. When this material dries and hardens it sort of resembles the web of a spider.

Parry Clover

This wildflower prefers rocky areas at alpine or subalpine elevations, so it often does not begin blooming until July.

Purple-Blue Flowers i Found

Be sure to write down which flower you saw, where you were, the date and anything else it will be fun to remember!

_____

_____

_____

_____

_____

_____

_____

_____

_____

_____

Orange-Red Flowers

Indian Paintbrush

This is the Wyoming State Flower. Paintbrushes are the type of wildflower where the actual flower is not the colored part, but another very small part of the plant. The colored parts, or bracts, hide the true flower.

Fairy Trumpet

Red flowers are not that common, and the Fairy Trumpet is one of the most beautiful. It can be seen at almost any elevation. It is also known as Skunk Flower because if the stems and leaves are crushed, they smell like skunk! Hummingbirds love these flowers.

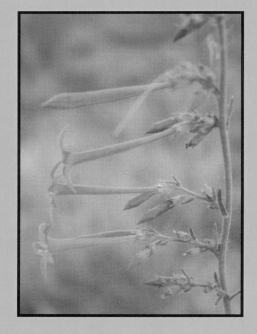

Orange-Red Flowers

King's Crown

This beautiful flower has thick fleshy leaves and can be found in Alpine areas as well as some lower elevations. It is also called Western Roseroot because the roots are reddish in color.

Spotted Coral Root

The Spotted Coral Root is an interesting orchid. It has no leaves or chlorophyll which most plants use to make the food they need to grow. This plant grows on a fungus, and that makes the nutrients the plant needs.

Orange-Red Flowers

Dusky Beardtongue

Can you see the hairs on the lower "tongue" of each of the flowers? That's where the Beardtongue name comes in. This type of flower is also called a Penstemon, which is a group of flowers that has several varieties and colors.

Orange Paintbrush

This is one of the larger Paintbrush wildflowers, and its color is very vibrant. You can often spot this flower along the roads that wind through the foothills.

Orange-Red Flowers

Copper Mallow

This plant is also known as Cowboy's Delight. It is common along the roadsides and in the fields of the plains and foothills. It has silvery hairy leaves and stems.

Wood Lily

There is usually one bloom per plant, and the blooms can be up to four inches across. These beautiful lilies are tempting to pick and so they are becoming more rare.

Orange-Red Flowers
I Found

Be sure to write down which flower you saw, where you were, the date and anything else it will be fun to remember!

_____

_____

_____

_____

_____

_____

_____

_____

_____

_____

_____

Ivory & White Flowers

Alpine Pussytoes

Pussytoes? That's a funny name! But when you see a cat's paw you can understand why it is named Pussytoes. It is also sometimes called Alpine Catspaw.

Scorpionweed

I think you can easily see how this wildflower resembles the tail of a scorpion. The flowers are tightly clustered on the curled stem. These plants can be more than two feet tall.

Ivory & White Flowers

Yucca

This plant is also known as Spanish Bayonet, and is the New Mexico state flower.

Monument Plant

This is a very interesting plant that can live twenty to eighty years. It typically flowers only once and then dies. These plants can grow to be six to eight feet tall.

Ivory & White Flowers

Arctic Gentian

This little alpine flower has purple stripes and usually is found near water.

Snowball Saxifrage

Doesn't this flower look like a snowball on a stick? This unusual name is one of my favorites to say. Saxifrage comes from Latin and means "stone breaker."

Ivory & White Flowers

Miner's Candle

These plants can be nearly two feet tall and they are common in dry fields and meadows, as well as along the sides of canyons. When the stems are full of white flowers they really resemble candles.

Ivory & White Flowers

Kinnikinnik

Kinnikinnick is a fun name to say. It is a Native American word that means "something to smoke." The leaves were dried and used as tobacco or mixed in with it and smoked in pipes.

Common Mouse Ear

Can you see the mouse ears? These delicate flowers are common along lower trails.

Ivory & White Flowers I Found

Be sure to write down which flower you saw, where you were, the date and anything else it will be fun to remember!

_____

_____

_____

_____

_____

_____

_____

_____

_____

_____

Penstemon

Learn More!

If you want to learn more about Rocky Mountain Wildflowers, there are several good references including books and web sites. The following is a partial list:

Guide to Colorado Wildflowers, Volume 1 & 2 by G. K. Guennel

Rocky Mountain Flora by James Ells

Wildflowers of the Rocky Mountains by George W. Scotter and Halle Flygate

Colorado Rocky Mountain Wildflowers presented by Denver Plants www.denverplants.com/wflwr/index.htm.

Southwest Colorado Wildflowers www.swcoloradowildflowers.com

Colorado State University Herbarium Wildflower Photos http://herbarium.biology.colostate.edu/photo.htm

Celebrating Wildflowers by the US Forest Service http://www.fs.fed.us/wildflowers/index.shtml

A more extensive collection of author Mary Dubler's wildflower photographs is found at www.wildflowersofcolorado.com.

Water Lilies on Fern Lake in Rocky Mountain National Park

LaVergne, TN USA
02 December 2009
165687LV00001B